MASONRY
ESSENTIALS

BLACK & DECKER ®

QUICK STEPS ™

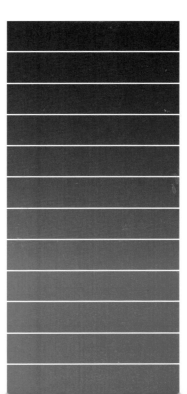

COWLES
Creative Publishing

A Division of Cowles Enthusiast Media, Inc.

Credits

Copyright © 1997
Cowles Creative Publishing, Inc.
Formerly Cy DeCosse Incorporated
5900 Green Oak Drive
Minnetonka, Minnesota 55343
1-800-328-3895
All rights reserved
Printed in U.S.A.

COWLES
Creative Publishing
A Division of Cowles Enthusiast Media, Inc.

President/COO: Nino Tarantino
Executive V.P./Editor-in-Chief: William B. Jones

Created by: The Editors of Cowles Creative Publishing, Inc.,
in cooperation with Black & Decker.  is
a trademark of the Black & Decker Corporation and is
used under license.

Printed on American paper by:
 Quebecor Printing
 99 98 97 96 / 5 4 3 2 1

COWLES
Enthusiast Media

President/COO: Philip L. Penny

Books available in this series:

Wiring Essentials
Plumbing Essentials
Carpentry Essentials
Painting Essentials
Flooring Essentials
Landscape Essentials
Masonry Essentials
Door & Window Essentials
Roof & Siding Essentials
Deck Essentials
Porch & Patio Essentials
Built-In Essentials

Contents

Tools for mixing concrete and for site preparation include: a sturdy wheelbarrow (A) with a minimum capacity of 6 cubic ft.; a power concrete mixer (B) for larger poured concrete projects (more than ½ cubic yard); a masonry hoe (C); a mortar box (D) for mixing mortar and small amounts of concrete; a square-end spade (E) for removing sod by hand, excavating, and for settling poured concrete; a sod cutter (F) for stripping larger areas of sod for reuse; and a tamper (G) for compacting the building site and subbase.

Masonry Tools

Masonry is a great building material for making long-lasting improvements to your home. Brick, block, and concrete provide an attractive appearance and texture to outdoor projects. Masonry can often seem intimidating at first, but with the information in this book, the average do-it-yourselfer can master basic techniques and learn valuable maintenance tips. To work effectively with masonry products, you will need to buy or rent some special-purpose tools.

Trowels, floats, edgers, and jointers are hand tools used to place, shape, and finish concrete and mortar. Bricksets and cold chisels are used to cut and fit brick and block. Equip your circular saw and power drill with cutting discs designed for use with concrete and brick to convert them into special-purpose masonry tools.

For most poured concrete projects, a power concrete mixer is a valuable tool. If the project requires more than one cubic yard of concrete, having the concrete delivered in ready-mix form will save time and ensure consistency. For small projects and for mixing mortar, a mortar box and masonry hoe can be used effectively.

Specialty masonry tools for handling concrete, mortar, and masonry units include: a magnesium float (A) for setting exposed aggregate or smoothing concrete to a hard, glossy finish; a wood float (B) for smoothing most exterior masonry surfaces; a groover (C) for cutting control joints into concrete; a stair edger (D) for creating smooth, even noses on steps; an edger (E) for rounding off edges in concrete at form locations; a jointer (F) for smoothing mortar joints; a power drill (G) with masonry bits (H) and a masonry grinding disc (I); a masonry-cutting blade for a circular saw (J); a masonry trowel (K) for building with brick or block; a pointing trowel (L) for repairing masonry; a brickset (M) for cutting brick and block; a cold chisel (N) for chipping out and breaking apart masonry; a bricklayer's hammer (O) with a claw for cutting masonry units; a maul (P) for driving form stakes and for use with a cold chisel and brickset.

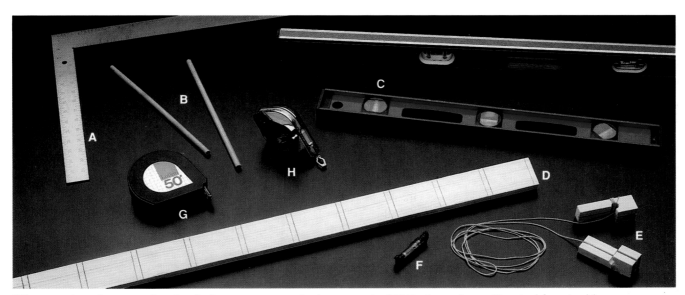

Alignment and measuring tools for masonry projects include: a carpenter's framing square (A) for setting project outlines; ⅜" dowels (B) for use as spacers between dry-laid masonry units; levels (C) for setting forms and for use when stacking masonry units; a story pole (D) that can be calibrated for stacking masonry units; line blocks and mason's string (E) for stacking brick and block; a line level (F) for making layouts and setting slope; a tape measure (G); and a chalkline (H) for marking layout lines on footing or slabs.

Safety & Disposal

Concrete products must be handled with care and disposed of properly. Concrete and mortar mix contains silica, which is a hazardous substance in large quantities, so always wear a particle mask when handling or mixing dry mix, and read and follow the manufacturer's safety precautions. Because these products will irritate your skin, always wear gloves when handling masonry products.

Concrete products are heavy, and lifting and moving them is hard work. For added protection, and when lifting, always wear a lifting belt and take care to use safe lifting techniques.

Most waste-removal companies will not accept masonry waste in regular curbside pickup. You will need to make special pickup arrangements—call your waste-disposal company for information. Where possible, use old masonry waste as clean fill for new projects.

Wear protective equipment, including a particle mask, eyewear, and gloves when mixing masonry products. Concrete products can be health hazards, and they will irritate skin upon contact. Also wear a mask to protect yourself from dust when cutting concrete, brick, or block.

Tips for Working Safely

Wear a lifting belt to help prevent lower back strain when stacking brick and block, and when hand-mixing concrete products. Always lift with your legs, not your back, and keep the items being lifted as close to your body as you can.

Keep the job site clean and well organized by creating a storage area for tools and by removing dirt and debris from the worksite immediately. NOTE: Always use a GFCI extension cord when working with power tools outdoors.

Tips for Working at Heights

Anchor your ladder at the top and bottom, using rope and a screw eye at the top, and stakes at the bottom. Do not carry heavy items up ladders—use a rope and pulley.

Use rented scaffolding for projects that require extended time working at heights, like tuckpointing a chimney. Scaffolding provides a much safer working platform, and is easier on the legs than a ladder. Get safety and operating instructions from the rental store if you have never used scaffolding before. Always make sure the feet of the scaffolding are level and secure (inset).

Tips for Disposal

Save old broken-up concrete for use as clean fill in building and landscaping projects.

Reuse sod by removing it carefully from the project area with a sod cutter (available for rent at most rental stores) or a square-end spade. Roll up the sod carefully, and lay it as soon as possible in another area of your yard.

Too dry

Too wet

Correct

Concrete Basics

If you are mixing concrete on-site, you have two options: you can purchase the ingredients separately and blend them together to achieve a mixture suited for your project. Or, you can purchase bags of pre-mixed concrete, and simply add water. For most projects around the home, buying pre-mixed products is a better choice. Premixed concrete yields uniform results, and it is fast and easy to use.

For smaller projects, a wheelbarrow or mortar box is an adequate mixing container. But for larger projects, consider renting or buying a power mixer, or have the concrete delivered by a ready-mix company.

A good mixture of concrete is crucial to any successful concrete project. Properly mixed concrete is damp enough to form in your hand when you squeeze, but not so damp that it loses its shape quickly. If the mixture is too dry, the aggregate will be too hard to work, and will not smooth out easily for an even, finished appearance. A wet mixture will slide off the trowel, and may cause cracking and other defects in the finished surface.

Components of Concrete

The basic ingredients of concrete are the same, whether the concrete is mixed from scratch, purchased premixed, or delivered by a ready-mix company. Portland cement is the bonding agent. It contains crushed lime and cement, and other bonding minerals. Sand and a combination of aggregates add volume and strength to the mix. Water is used to activate the cement. It evaporates to allow the concrete to dry into a solid mass. By varying the ratios of the ingredients, professionals can create concrete with special properties that are suited for specific situations.

Premixed concrete products contain all the components of concrete. Just add water, mix, and you are ready to pour. Usually sold in 60-lb. bags that yield approximately ½ cu. ft., these products are available in different forms with specific properties for specific applications. *General-purpose concrete mix* is usually the most inexpensive product, and is suitable for most do-it-yourself, poured concrete projects. *Fiber-reinforced concrete mix* contains strands of fiberglass that increase strength. For some applications, you can use fiber-reinforced concrete instead of general-purpose concrete to eliminate the need for metal reinforcement. *High-early premixed concrete* contains accelerating agents that cause it to set quickly—a desirable property if you are pouring when temperatures are cold. *Sand mix* contains no mixed aggregate, and is used in repairs and in casting projects where larger aggregate is not desirable.

Tips for Estimating Concrete

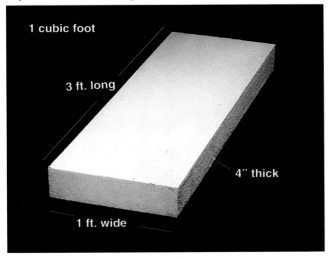

1 cubic foot
3 ft. long
4" thick
1 ft. wide

Concrete Coverage		
Volume	Thickness	Surface Coverage
1 cu. yd.	2"	160 sq. ft.
1 cu. yd.	3"	110 sq. ft.
1 cu. yd.	4"	80 sq. ft
1 cu. yd.	5"	65 sq. ft.
1 cu. yd.	6"	55 sq. ft.
1 cu. yd.	8"	40 sq. ft.

Measure the width and length of the project in feet, then multiply the dimensions to get the square footage. Measure the thickness in feet (4" thick equals ⅓ ft.), then multiply the square footage times the thickness to get the cubic footage. For example, 1 ft. × 3 ft. × ⅓ ft. = 1 cu. ft. Twenty-seven cubic feet equals one cubic yard.

Coverage rates for poured concrete are determined by the thickness of the slab you pour. The same volume of concrete will yield less surface area if the thickness of the slab is increased. The chart above shows the relationship between slab thickness, surface area, and volume.

How to Mix Concrete by Hand

1 Empty contents of premixed concrete bags into a mortar box, wheelbarrow, or another large container. Form a hollow in the pile of dry mix, then pour water into the hollow. Start with 1 gallon of clean tapwater per 60-lb. bag.

2 Work with a hoe, continuing to add water until a good consistency is achieved (page 8). Clear out any dry pockets from the corners. Do not overwork the mix. Also, keep track of how much water you use in the first batch so you will have a reliable recipe for subsequent batches.

How to Mix Concrete with a Power Mixer

1 Fill a bucket with 1 gallon of water for each 60-lb. bag of concrete you will use in the batch (for most power mixers, 3 bags is workable). Pour in half the water. Before you start power-mixing, review the operating instructions carefully.

2 Add all of the dry concrete mix in the batch, then the rest of the water. Mix for a minute. Pour in water as needed until the proper consistency is achieved (page 8), and mix for 3 minutes. Pivot the mixing drum to empty the concrete into a wheelbarrow. Rinse out the drum immediately.

Have ready-mix concrete delivered for large projects. Prepare the site and build the forms yourself, and try to have helpers on hand to help you place and tool the concrete when it arrives.

Ordering Ready-mix Concrete

For large concrete jobs (1 cubic yard or more), have ready-mix concrete delivered to your site. Although it is more expensive, it saves time. Seek referrals, and check your telephone directory under "Concrete" for ready-mix sources.

Tips for preparing for concrete delivery:
- Fully prepare the building site (pages 12 to 17).

- Discuss your project with the experts at the ready-mix company. They will help you decide how much and what type of concrete you need. To help you determine your quantity needs, see the chart on page 9.

- Call the supplier the day before the scheduled pour to confirm the quantity and delivery time.

- Read the receipt you get from the driver. It will tell you at what time the concrete was mixed. Before you accept the concrete, make sure no more than 90 minutes has elapsed between the time it was mixed and the time it was delivered.

Prepare a clear delivery path to the project site, so when the truck rolls up you are ready to pour. Lay planks over the forms and subbase to make a roadway for the wheelbarrows or concrete hoppers. If you have an asphalt driveway, or a concrete driveway that is cracking, have the truck park on the street to prevent driveway damage.

Preparing the Project Site

The basic steps in preparing a project site are: lay out a design using stakes and strings to outline the project; clear the project area and strip off sod; excavate the site to allow for a subbase or a footing, if needed, and the concrete; pour footings or lay a subbase for drainage and stability; build and install wooden forms with reinforcement in place.

Site preparation depends on the type of project and the condition of the site. Plan on using a subbase of compactible gravel. Some projects require footings that extend past the frostline, while others, like sidewalks, do not. Adding metal reinforcement to the project is not always required, but is a good idea. Check with your local building department for guidelines.

Projects built on heavily sloped sites normally require grading of the soil prior to pouring concrete. If your yard slope is more than 1" per ft., you may need to add or remove soil to create a level building surface; contact a landscape engineer or a building inspector for advice on how to modify your yard to accommodate your masonry project.

SAFETY TIP: Beware of buried electric and gas lines when digging. Contact your local public utility company before you start digging.

Everything You Need:

Tools: rope, hand maul, tape measure, mason's string, line level, spade, sod cutter, wheelbarrow, shovel, tamper.

Materials: 2 × 4 lumber, 3" screws, compactible gravel.

Tips for Preparing the Project Site

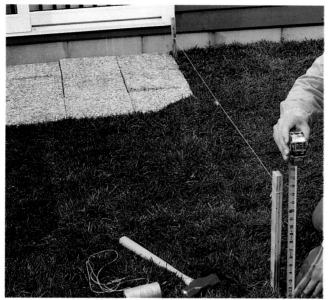

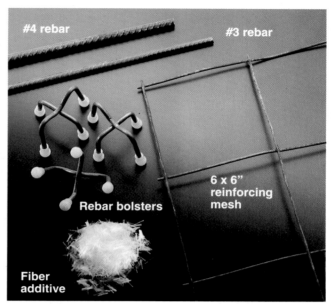

Measure the slope of the building site to determine if you need to do grading work before you start your project. First, drive stakes at each end of the project area. Attach a mason's string between the stakes and use a line level to set it at level. At each stake, measure from the string to the ground. The difference in the distances (in inches), when divided by the distance between stakes (in ft.) will give you the slope (in inches per foot). If the slope is greater than 1" per foot, you likely will need to regrade the building site.

Reinforcement materials: *Metal rebar,* available in sizes ranging from #2 (⅛" diameter) to #5 (⅝" diameter) is used to reinforce narrow concrete slabs, like sidewalks, and in masonry walls. For most projects, #3 rebar (⅜" diameter) is suitable. *Wire mesh* (sometimes called re-mesh) is most common in 6 × 6" grids. It is usually used for broad surfaces, like patios. Rebar and wire mesh are suspended off the subbase by *bolsters.* *Fiber additive* is mixed into concrete to strengthen small projects that receive little traffic.

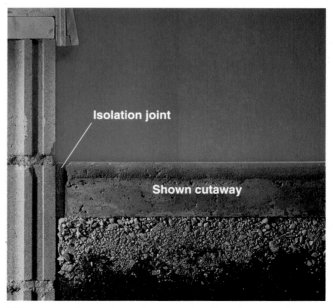

Add a compactible gravel subbase to provide a level, stable foundation for the concrete. The compactible gravel also improves drainage—an important consideration if you are building on soil that is high in clay content. For most building projects, pour a layer of compactible gravel about 5" thick, and use a tamper to compress it to 4" (photo, previous page).

When pouring concrete next to structures, glue a ½"-thick asphalt-impregnated fibrous board, called an isolation board, to the adjoining structure to keep the concrete from bonding with the structure. The board creates an isolation joint, allowing the two structures to move independently, minimizing the risk of cracking.

How to Lay Out & Excavate a Building Site

1 Lay out a rough project outline with a rope or hose. Use a carpenter's square to set perpendicular lines. To create the actual layout, begin by driving wood stakes near each corner of the rough layout. The goal is to arrange the stakes so they are outside the actual project area, but are in alignment with the borders of the project (if you extended the project outlines 1 ft. in each direction, the stakes would be at each of the eight endpoints). NOTE: Projects built next to permanent structures should use the structure to define one project side.

2 Connect the stakes with mason's strings. The strings should follow the actual project outlines. To make sure the strings are square, use the 3-4-5 triangle method: measure and mark points 3 ft. out from one corner along one string, and 4 ft. out along the intersecting string at the corner. Measure between the points, and adjust the positions of the strings until the distance between the points is exactly 5 ft.

3 Reset the stakes, if necessary, to conform to the positions of the squared strings. Check all corners with the 3-4-5 method, and adjust until the entire project area is exactly square. This can be a lengthy process with plenty of trial and error, but it is very important to the success of the project, especially if you plan to build on the concrete surface.

Line level

4 Attach a line level to one of the mason's strings to use as a reference. Adjust the string up or down as necessary until it is level. Adjust the other strings until they are level, making sure that intersecting strings contact one another (this ensures that they are all at the same height relative to ground level).

5 Most concrete surfaces should have a slight slope to direct water runoff, especially if they are near your house. To create a slope, shift the level mason's strings on opposite sides of the project downward on their stakes (the lower end should be farther away from the house). To create a standard slope of ⅛" per foot, multiply the distance between the stakes on one side (in ft.) by ⅛. For example, if the stakes are 10 ft. apart, the result will be ¹⁰⁄₈ (1¼"). Move the strings down that much on the stakes on the low ends.

6 Start excavating the project site by removing the sod. Use a sod cutter if you wish to reuse the sod elsewhere in your yard (lay the sod as soon as possible). Otherwise, use a square-end spade to cut away sod. Strip off the sod at least 6" outside the mason's strings to make room for 2 × 4 forms.

7 Make a story pole as a guide for excavating the site. First, measure down to ground level from the high end of a slope line. Add 7½" to that distance (4" for the subbase material and 3½" for the concrete if you are using 2 × 4 forms). Mark the total distance on the story pole, measuring from one end. Remove soil in the project site with a spade. Use the story pole to make sure the bottom of the site is the same distance from the slope line at all points as you dig.

8 Lay a subbase for the project (unless your project requires a frost footing). Pour a 5"-thick layer of compactible gravel in the project site, and tamp until the gravel is even and compressed to 4" in depth. NOTE: The subbase should extend at least 6" beyond the project outline.

How to Build & Install Wood Forms

1 A form is a frame, usually made from 2 × 4 lumber, laid around a project site to contain and shape freshly poured concrete. Cut the 2 × 4s to create a frame with inside dimensions equal to the total size of the project. Gang-cut same-sized boards to save time.

2 Use the mason's strings that outline the project (pages 14 to 15) as a reference for setting form boards in place. Starting with the longest form board, position the boards so the inside edges are directly below the strings.

3 Cut several 12"-long pieces of 2 × 4 to use as form stakes, and trim one end of each stake to create a sharp point. Drive the stakes at the outside edges of the form boards, spaced at 3-ft. intervals, and directly behind any joints in the form boards.

4 Drive 3" deck screws through the stakes and into one of the form boards. Set a level so it spans the staked form and the opposite form board, and use the level as a guide for staking the second form board so it is level with the first (for large projects, use the mason's strings as the primary guide for setting the height of all form boards).

5 Stake the rest of the form boards to complete the frame. With the tops of all form boards level, drive 3" deck screws at all corner joints to bond the form frame together. Coat the forms with vegetable oil before you pour concrete. TIP: Tack nails or drive screws into the sides of the forms to mark the control joint locations, saving time during the pour.

Variations for Building Forms

Use plywood (top left photo) for building taller forms for projects like concrete steps (pages 30 to 35). Gang-cut plywood form sides, and brace with 2 × 4 arms attached to 2 × 4 cleats at the sides.
Use the earth as a form (bottom left photo) when building footings for poured concrete building proj-

ects (page 37). Use standard 2 × 4 forms for the tops of footings for building with brick or block.
Create curves (above, right) with ⅛"-thick hardboard attached at the inside corners of a form frame. Drive support stakes behind the curved form.

Tips for Laying Metal Reinforcement

Cut metal rebar with a reciprocating saw that is equipped with a metal-cutting blade (cutting metal rebar with a hacksaw can take 5 to 10 minutes per cut). Use wire cutters to cut wire mesh.

Overlap joints in metal rebar by at least 12", then bind the ends together with heavy-gauge wire. Overlap seams in wire mesh reinforcement by 12".

Stay at least 1" away from forms with the edges or ends of metal reinforcement. Use bolsters or small chunks of concrete to raise metal reinforcement off the subbase, but make sure it is at least 2" below the tops of the forms.

Placing Concrete

Placing concrete involves delivering fresh concrete from the source into forms, then beveling and smoothing the concrete with a variety of masonry tools. Once the surface is smoothed and level, control joints are cut and the edges of the project are rounded off for a finished look. Because placing and tooling directly affect the outward appearance of any concrete building project, it is important that you do careful work.

Everything You Need:

Tools: wheelbarrow, hoe, spade, hammer, trowel, wood float, groover, edger.

Materials: concrete, 2 × 4 lumber, mixing container, water container.

Start pouring concrete at the farthest point from the concrete source, and work your way back.

Tips for Pouring Concrete

Do not overload your wheelbarrow. Experiment with sand or dry mix before mixing concrete to find a comfortable, controllable volume. This also helps you get a feel for how many wheelbarrow loads it will take to complete your project.

Lay planks over the forms to make a ramp for the wheelbarrow. Avoid disturbing the building site by using ramp supports (above). Make sure you have a flat, stable surface between the concrete source and the forms.

How to Place Concrete

1 Load the wheelbarrow with fresh concrete. Make sure you have a clear path from the source to the site. Always load wheelbarrows from the front. Loading wheelbarrows from the sides can cause tipping.

2 Pour concrete in evenly spaced loads (each load is called a "pod"). Start at the end farthest from the concrete source, and pour so the top of the pod is a few inches above the tops of the forms. Do not pour too close to the forms. NOTE: If you are using a ramp, stay clear of the end of the ramp.

3 Continue to place concrete pods next to preceding pods, working away from the first pod. Do not pour more concrete than you can tool at one time. Keep an eye on the concrete to make sure it does not harden before you can start tooling.

4 Distribute concrete evenly in the project area, using a masonry hoe. Work the concrete with a hoe until it is roughly flat, and the surface is slightly above the tops of the forms.

(continued next page)

5 Work the blade of a spade between the inside edges of the form and the concrete to remove trapped air bubbles that can weaken concrete.

6 Rap the forms with a hammer or the blade of the shovel to help settle the concrete. This also draws finer aggregates in the concrete against the forms, creating a smoother surface on the sides. (This is especially important when building steps.)

7 Use a screed board—a straight piece of 2 × 4 long enough to rest on opposite forms—to strike off the excess concrete. Move the screed board in a sawing motion from left to right, and keep the screed flat as you work. If screeding leaves any valleys in the surface, add fresh concrete in the low areas and screed to level.

8 Precut control joints (page 16, step 5) at pre-marked locations with a mason's trowel, using a straightedge as a guide. Control joints are cut into the concrete surface (see step 10) to direct cracking in a direction that does not cause structural damage. Space the control joints evenly for a more attractive appearance.

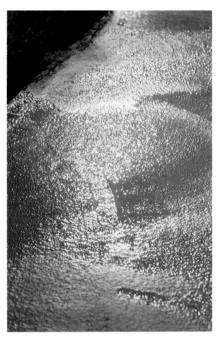

9 Use a wood float to smooth the surface. Float lightly, using an arcing motion, until the entire surface is smooth. Do not overfloat. NOTE: When tooling concrete, tip the lead edge of the tool upward slightly to prevent gouging.

TIP: Floating concrete causes puddles of water, called "bleed water," to form on the surface. Once bleed water forms, finish up any tooling as quickly as possible.

10 Allow the concrete to dry until the bleed water disappears. Then draw a groover across the precut control joints (step 8), using a straightedge as a guide. You may need to make several passes to create a smooth control joint.

11 Shape concrete with an edging tool between the forms and the concrete to create a smooth, finished appearance. You may need to make multiple passes. Use a wood float to smooth out any marks left by the edger or groover. Apply decorative finishes, if desired, then let the concrete cure (pages 22 and 23).

Finishing option: exposed aggregate. Sometimes called "seeding" concrete, applying decorative aggregate to the fresh concrete surface creates an attractive effect with many design options. The photo above shows what a few varieties of aggregate look like when they are used for an exposed-aggregate surface.

Finishing option: broomed finish. Create by dragging a stiff-bristled garage broom across a concrete surface immediately after tooling the concrete. Do not overwork the concrete.

Finishing & Curing Concrete

Finishing and curing concrete are critical last steps in any concrete project. Proper curing ensures that the concrete reaches its maximum strength and remains free of surface defects that can ruin the appearance. There are many theories on the best way to cure concrete, but for residential projects, simply covering the concrete with plastic is a simple and effective method.

Applying a decorative finish dresses up the plain appearance of concrete surfaces. Exposed-aggregate (or "seeded") finishes are common on walkways, patios, and other surfaces. Brooming is a good option for any surface that receives high traffic volume. Check around your neighborhood for other ideas for creative concrete finishes.

Everything You Need:
Tools: broom, wheelbarrow, shovel, wood float, hand broom, hose, coarse brush.
Materials: sheet plastic, "seeding" aggregate, water.

How to Cure Concrete

Use a plastic covering for curing concrete. Curing concrete keeps the water in the concrete from evaporating too quickly, which helps prevent surface defects. Cure for a week, covered with plastic. Anchor the plastic securely, and overlap and tape any seams.

How to Create an Exposed-aggregate Finish

1 After smoothing off the surface with a screed board (page 20), spread aggregate evenly over the surface with a shovel or by hand. Smaller aggregate (up to 1" in diameter) should be spread in a single-thickness layer; for larger seeding stones, try to maintain a separation between stones that is roughly equal to the size of one stone. NOTE: Always wash the aggregate thoroughly before seeding.

2 Float the seeded surface with a magnesium float until a thin layer of concrete rises up to completely cover the stones. Do not overfloat. TIP: Cover the surface with plastic to keep the concrete from hardening too quickly if you are seeding a large area.

3 As soon as the bleed water disappears, cut control joints and tool the edges (page 21). Let the concrete set for 30 to 60 minutes, then mist a section of the surface and scrub with a brush to remove the concrete covering the aggregate. If any stones dislodge, reset them and try again later. When you can scrub without dislodging stones, mist and scrub the entire surface to expose the aggregate. Rinse clean. Do not let the concrete dry too long, or it will be difficult to scrub off.

4 After the concrete has cured for one week (previous page), remove the covering and rinse the surface with a hose. If any cement residue remains, try scrubbing it clean. If scrubbing is ineffective, wash the surface with a muriatic acid solution, then rinse immediately and thoroughly with water. OPTION: After three weeks, apply exposed-aggregate sealer (pages 54 to 55).

An angled concrete walkway creates a functional link between two points, while adding a unique design element to your yard.

Walkways

If your house fills up with muddy footprints after every rainstorm, and a path of worn grass has developed in your yard, the chances are good that you need a walkway. Poured concrete is an ideal material for residential walkways since nothing matches it for permanence and resistance to damage from foot traffic or shoveling.

Always check with your local building department before starting a walkway project. This is especially important if you plan to build a walkway in the front of your house. Most areas closely regulate the construction of public-access sidewalks.

Tips for Planning:

• Design walkways to follow traffic flow, but bear in mind that a walkway can divide a yard. You may prefer to route the walkway closer to the edge of your property to preserve larger areas of your yard for recreational use.

• Build walkways that are the same width as other existing walkways (3 ft.and 4 ft. are common widths; 2 ft. is the recommended minimum width).

• A walkway can follow a gradual slope in a yard, but severe slopes require steps or regrading.

• Keep walkways at least 2 ft. away from trees. Damage from roots and tree trunks is a leading cause of concrete failure.

Tips for Directing Water Runoff on Walkways

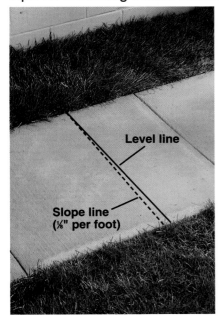

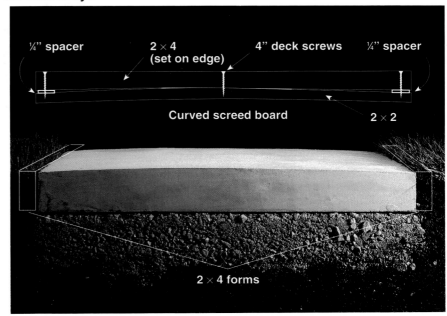

¼" spacer   2 × 4 (set on edge)   4" deck screws   ¼" spacer

Curved screed board   2 × 2

2 × 4 forms

Slope walkways away from the house to prevent water damage to the foundation or basement. Outline the location of the walkway with mason's strings, then lower the outer string to create a slope of ⅛" per ft. (see pages 14 to 15).

Crown the walkway so it is ¼" higher at the center than at the edges. This will prevent water from pooling on the surface. To make the crown, construct a curved screed board by cutting a 2 × 2 and a 2 × 4 long enough to rest on the walkway forms. Butt them together edge to edge and insert a spacer between them at each end. Attach the parts with 4" deck screws driven at the center and the edges. The 2 × 2 will be drawn up at the center, creating a curved edge. Smooth the concrete with the curved edge of the screed board facing down.

Tips for Designing Walkways

Use curves to add visual interest to an otherwise plain walkway or to add contrast to yards with mostly square features. Use the same construction techniques for straight or angled walkways, but use ⅛"-thick hardboard to make the curved forms (page 17).

Look for traffic patterns in your lawn to find the most logical location for a new walkway.

How to Build a Walkway

1 Select a rough layout for the walkway based on the design tips shown on page 24. For function and appearance, we chose to include an angled turn in our walkway. Stake out the location and connect the stakes with mason's strings. Set slope lines if needed (pages 14 to 15).

2 Remove sod in the project site and 6" beyond the outlines, then excavate the site with a spade, following the slope lines to maintain consistent depth (page 15).

3 Pour a 5"-thick layer of compactible gravel into the site to create a subbase for the walkway. Tamp the subbase until it compacts to 4" thick and it is even on the surface (page 15).

4 Build and install forms made out of 2 × 4 boards set on edge (page 16). Miter-cut the ends at angled joints. Position them so the inside edges are lined up with the strings, then drive 2 × 4 stakes next to the forms at 3-ft. intervals. Attach the stakes to the forms with 3" deck screws. Use a carpenter's level to make sure the forms are level to one another. Drive a stake at each side of angled form joints.

5 Glue an isolation board (page 13) to steps, the house foundation, or other permanent structures that adjoin the walkway.

OPTION: Reinforce the walkway with #3 steel rebar (page 17). For a 3-ft.-wide walkway, lay two sections of rebar spaced evenly inside the project area. Use bolsters to support the rebar (make sure bolsters are at least 2" below the tops of the forms). Bend rebar to follow any angles or curves, and overlap pieces at angled joints by 12". Mark locations for control joints (to be cut with a groover later) by tacking nails to the outside faces of the forms, spaced roughly at 3-ft. intervals.

(continued next page)

6 Mix, then pour concrete into the project area (pages 18 to 19). Use a masonry hoe to spread it evenly within the forms. After pouring all of the concrete, run a spade along the inside edges of the form, then rap the outside edges of the forms with a hammer to help settle the concrete.

7 Build a curved screed board (page 25) and use it to form a crown when you smooth out the concrete (page 20). NOTE: A helper makes this easier.

8 Smooth the surface with a wood float (page 21). Precut control joints at marked locations (page 20) using a trowel and a straightedge. Let the concrete dry until the bleed water disappears (page 21).

9 Shape the edges of the concrete by running an edger along the forms. Smooth out any marks created by the edger with a float. Lift the leading edges of the edger and float slightly as you work.

10 Cut control joints using a groover and a straightedge as a guide. Use a float to smooth out any tool marks.

11 Create a textured, non-skid surface by drawing a clean, stiff-bristled broom across the surface. Avoid overlapping broom marks. Cover the walkway with plastic and let the concrete cure for one week (pages 22 to 23).

12 Remove the forms, then backfill the space at the sides of the walkway with dirt or sod. Seal the concrete, if desired (pages 54 to 55), according to the manufacturer's directions.

Brand-new concrete steps give a fresh, clean appearance to your house. And if your old steps are unstable, replacing them with concrete steps that have a non-skid surface will create a safer living environment.

Concrete Steps

Replacing old, cracked or damaged steps with sturdy concrete steps will make your home a safer place for your family and for visitors.

Designing steps requires some math work and a fair amount of trial and error. The basic idea is to come up with a design that fits the space while following practical safety guidelines. You can adjust different elements, such as the landing depth, and the height and depth of each step, as long as the steps meet recommended safety guidelines. Sketching your plan on paper will make the job easier.

Before demolishing your old steps, measure them to see if they meet safety guidelines. If so, you can use them as a reference for your new steps. If not, start from scratch so your new steps do not repeat any design errors.

Step Safety Guidelines:

• *Landing depth* should be at least 12" more than the width of the door; *step treads* should be between 10" and 12" deep; *step risers* should be between 6" and 8" in height.

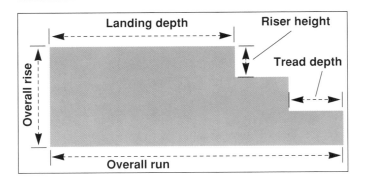

How to Design Steps

Overall run

1 Attach a mason's string to the house foundation, 1" below the bottom of the door threshold. Drive a stake where you want the base of the bottom step to fall. Attach the other end of the string to the stake and use a line level to level it. Measure the length of the string—this distance is the overall depth, or *run*, of the steps.

Overall rise

2 Measure down from the string to the bottom of the stake to determine the overall height, or *rise*, of the steps. Divide the overall rise by the estimated number of steps. The rise of each step should be between 6" and 8". For example, if the overall rise is 21" and you plan to build three steps, the rise of each step would be 7" (21 divided by 3), which falls within the recommended safety range for riser height.

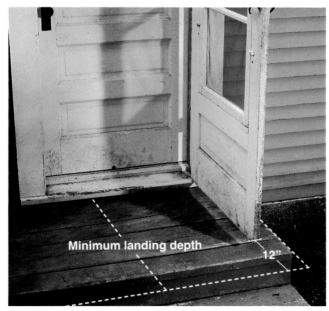

Minimum landing depth   12"

3 Measure the width of your door and add 12"; this number is the minimum depth you should plan for the landing area of the steps. The landing depth plus the depth of each step should fit within the overall run of the steps. If necessary, you can increase the overall run by moving the stake at the planned base of the steps away from the house, or by increasing the depth of the landing.

4 Sketch a detailed plan for the steps, keeping these guidelines in mind: each step should be 10" to 12" deep, with a riser height between 6" and 8", and the landing should be 12" deeper than the swing radius (width) of your door. Adjust the parts of the steps as needed, but stay within the given ranges. Creating a final sketch will take time, but it is worth doing carefully.

How to Build Concrete Steps

1 Remove or demolish existing steps; if the old steps are concrete, set aside the rubble to use as fill material for the new steps. Wear protective gear, including eye protection and gloves, when demolishing concrete.

2 Dig two 12"-wide trenches for the footings, at the required depth (pages 36 to 37). Locate the trenches perpendicular to the foundation, spaced so the footings will extend 3" wider than the outside edges of the finished steps. Install steel rebar grids (page 39) for reinforcement. Since they will support poured concrete, simply strike off the footings level with the ground, rather than building forms.

3 Mix the concrete and pour the footings. Smooth the concrete with a screed board (page 20). You do not need to float the surface afterwards.

4 When bleed water disappears (page 21), insert 12" sections of rebar 6" into the concrete, spaced at 12" intervals and centered side to side. Leave 1 ft. of clear space at each end.

5 Let the footings cure for two days, then excavate the area between them to 4" deep. Pour in a 5"-thick layer of compactible gravel subbase and tamp until it is level with the footings.

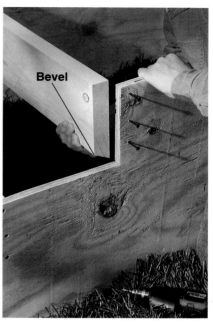

6 Transfer the measurements for the side forms from your working sketch onto ¾" exterior-grade plywood. Cut out the forms along the cutting lines, using a jig saw. Save time by clamping two pieces of plywood together and cutting both side forms at the same time. Add a ⅛" per ft. back-to-front slope to the landing part of the form.

Make slopes a minimum of ⅛" per foot

7 Cut form boards for the risers to fit between the side forms. Bevel the bottom edges of the boards when cutting to create clearance for the float at the back edges of the steps. Attach the riser forms to the side forms with 2" deck screws.

Bevel

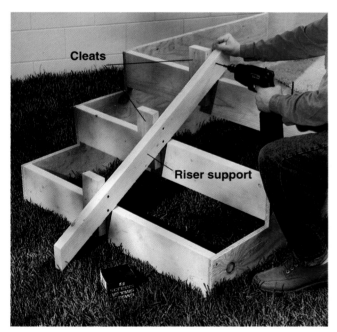

Cleats

Riser support

8 Cut a 2 × 4 to make a center support for the riser forms. Use 2" deck screws to attach cleats to the riser forms, then attach the support to the cleats. Check to make sure all corners are square.

9 Cut an isolation board (page 13) and glue it to the house foundation at the back of the project area. Set the form onto the footings, flush against the isolation board. Add 2 × 4 bracing arms to the sides of the form, and attach them to cleats on the sides and to stakes driven into the ground.

(continued next page)

10 Fill the form with clean fill (broken concrete or rubble). Stack the fill carefully, keeping it 6" away from the sides, back, and top edges of the form. Shovel smaller fragments onto the pile to fill the void areas.

11 Lay pieces of #3 metal rebar on top of the fill pile for reinforcement. Space the pieces at 12" intervals, and attach them to bolsters with wire to keep them from moving when the concrete is poured. Keep rebar at least 2" below the tops of the form.

12 Mix the concrete and start pouring the steps one at a time, beginning with the bottom step. Settle the concrete and smooth it with a screed board (pages 19 to 20). Press a piece of #3 rebar 1" down into the "nose" of each tread for reinforcement.

13 Float the steps with a wood float (page 21), working the front edge of the float underneath the beveled edge at the bottom of each riser form.

14 Pour concrete in the forms for the remaining steps and the landing, keeping an eye on the poured concrete as you work. Stop to float any concrete as soon as the bleed water disappears (page 21). Press rebar into the nose of each step.

OPTION: For railings with mounting plates that attach to sunken J-bolts, install the bolts before the concrete sets. Otherwise, choose railings with surface-mounted hardware (see step 16) that can be attached after the steps are completed.

Mounting plate

15 Once the concrete has set, shape the steps and the landing with a step edger, then float and sweep the surface with a stiff-bristled broom (pages 21 to 23).

16 Let the concrete cure for one week, then remove the form and install a handrail (check with your local building department for handrail requirements). Backfill the area around the base of the steps, and seal the concrete if desired.

Footings are required by most building codes for concrete or brick and block structures that adjoin other permanent structures. Structures taller than 3 ft. normally require a footing.

Footing

Footings provide a stable, level base for brick, block, or poured concrete structures. They distribute the weight of the structure evenly, prevent sinking, and keep structures from moving during freezing and thawing.

The required depth of a footing is usually determined by the "frost line," which varies by region. The frost line is the point nearest ground level where the soil does not freeze. In colder climates, it is likely to be 48" or deeper. Frost footings (footings designed to keep structures from moving during freezing temperatures) should be built 12" deeper than the frost line for the area. Check with your local building department to find the frost line depth for your area.

Tips for Planning:

• Describe the structure you intend to build to your local building inspector to find out if it requires a footing, and if the footing needs reinforcement.

• Keep footings separate from adjoining structures by installing an isolation board (page 13).

• For smaller poured concrete projects, consider pouring the footing and the structure as one unit.

• In some cases, slab footings can be used, as long as the subbase provides adequate drainage.

• Footings generally are not built with a slope.

Options for Forming Footings

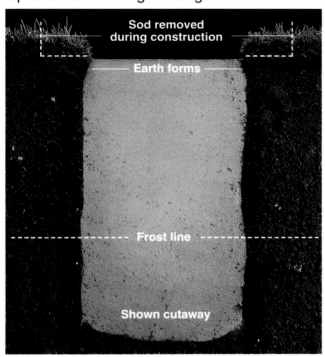

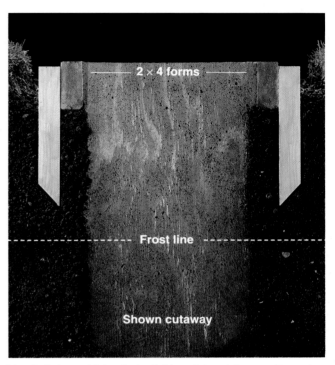

For poured concrete, use the earth as a form. Strip sod from around the project area, then strike off the concrete with screed board resting on the earth at the edges of the top of the trench.

For brick and block, build level 2 × 4 forms. Rest the screed board on the frames when you strike off the concrete to create a flat, even surface for stacking masonry units.

Tips for Building Footings

Make footings twice as wide as the width of the wall or structure they will support. They also should extend at least 12" past the ends of the project area.

Add tie-rods if you will be pouring concrete over the footing. After the concrete sets up, press 12" sections of rebar 6" into the concrete. The tie-rods will anchor the footing to the structure it will support.

How to Pour a Footing

1 Make a rough outline of the footing, using a rope or hose. Outline the project area with stakes and mason's strings (page 14).

2 Strip away sod 6" outside the project area on all sides, then excavate the trench for the footing to a depth 1 ft. below the frostline.

3 Build and install a 2 × 4 form frame for the footing, aligning it with the mason's strings (page 16). Stake the form in place, and adjust to level.

VARIATION: If your project abuts another structure, like a house foundation, slip a piece of fiber board into the trench to create an isolation joint between the footing and the structure (page 13).

4 Make two #3 rebar grids to reinforce the footing. For each grid, cut two pieces of #3 rebar 8" shorter than the length of the footing, and two pieces 4" shorter than the depth of the footing. Bind the pieces together with 16-gauge wire, forming a rectangle. Set the rebar grids upright in the trench, leaving 4" of space between the grids and the walls of the trench. Coat the inside edge of the form with vegetable oil.

5 Mix and pour concrete into the trench, filling it up to the top edges of the forms (pages 18 to 21). Strike off the concrete, using a 2 × 4 as a screed board. Add tie-rods if needed (page 37). Float the surface.

6 Cure the concrete for at least two days (one week is better) before you build on the footing. Remove the forms and backfill the area around the edges of the footing.

Good repairs restore both the appearance and the function to failing concrete structures and surfaces. Careful work can produce a well-blended, successful repair, like the one shown above.

Repairing Concrete Structures

Concrete is one of the most durable building materials, but it still requires repair and maintenance occasionally. Freezing and thawing, improper finishing techniques, a poor subbase, or lack of reinforcement all can cause problems with concrete. By addressing problems as soon as you discover them, you can prevent further damage that may be difficult or impossible to fix.

Concrete repair projects fall into a wide range, from simple cleaning and sealing, to completely removing and replacing sections of concrete. Filling cracks and repairing surface damage are the most common concrete repairs.

Another effective repair is resurfacing—covering an old concrete surface with fresh concrete. It is a good option for spalling, crazing, or popouts—minor problems that affect the appearance more than the structure. These problems often result from inadequate preparation or incorrect finishing techniques.

As with any kind of repair, the success of the project depends largely on good preparation and use of the best repair products for the job. Specially formulated repair products are manufactured for just about every type of concrete repair. Be sure to read the product-use information before purchasing any products; some products need to be used in combination with others.

A good repair can outlast the rest of the structure in some cases, but if structural damage has occurred, repairing the concrete is only a temporary solution. By using the right products and techniques, however, you can make cosmetic repairs that improve the appearance of the surface and keep damage from worsening.

This section shows:

- Identifying Concrete Problems (pages 42 to 43)
- Filling Cracks (pages 44 to 45)
- Patching Holes (pages 46 to 47)
- Resurfacing Concrete (pages 48 to 49)
- Repairing Steps (pages 50 to 51)
- Miscellaneous Concrete Repairs (pages 52 to 53)
- Sealing & Maintaining Concrete (pages 54 to 55)

Concrete Repair Products

Concrete repair products include: vinyl-reinforced concrete patch (A) for filling holes, popouts, and larger cracks; hydraulic cement (B) for repairing foundations, retaining walls, and other damp areas; quick-setting cement (C) for repairing vertical surfaces and unusual shapes; anchoring cement (D) for setting hardware in concrete; concrete sealing products (E); concrete recoating product (F) for creating a fresh surface on old concrete; masonry paint (G); joint-filler caulk (H); pour-in crack sealer (I); concrete cleaner (J); concrete fortifier (K) to strengthen concrete; bonding adhesive (L) to prepare the repair area; and concrete sand mix (M) for general repairs and resurfacing.

Tips for Disguising Repairs

Add concrete pigment to concrete patching compound to create a color that matches the original concrete. Experiment with different mixtures of pigment and repair cement until you find the right mixture. Samples should be dry to show the actual colors.

Use masonry paint to cover concrete repairs. Paint can be used on vertical or horizontal surfaces, but high-traffic surfaces will require more frequent touchup or repainting.

Widespread cracks all the way through the surface, and other forms of substantial damage, are very difficult to repair effectively. If the damage to the concrete is extensive, remove and replace the structure.

Identifying Concrete Problems

There are two general types of concrete failure: structural failure usually resulting from outside forces like freezing water; and surface damage most often caused by improper finishing techniques or concrete mixtures that do not have the right ratio of water to cement. Surface problems sometimes can be treated with permanent repairs if the correct products and techniques are used. More significant damage can be patched for cosmetic purposes and to resist further damage, but the structure may eventually need to be replaced.

Common Concrete Problems

Sunken concrete is usually caused by erosion of the subbase. Some structures, like sidewalks, can be raised to repair the subbase, then relaid. A more common (and more reliable) solution is to hire a mudjacking contractor to raise the surface by injecting fresh concrete below the surface.

Frost heave is common in colder climates. Frozen ground forces concrete slabs upward, and sections of the slab can pop up. The best solution is to break off and remove the affected section or sections, repair the subbase, and pour new sections that are set off by isolation joints (page 13).

Moisture buildup occurs in concrete structures, like foundations and retaining walls, that are in constant ground contact. To identify the moisture source, tape a piece of foil to the wall. If moisture collects on the outer surface of the foil, the source likely is condensation, which can be corrected by installing a dehumidifier. If moisture is not visible on the foil, it is likely seeping through the wall. Consult a professional mason.

Staining can ruin the appearance of a concrete surface or structure. Stains can be removed with commercial-grade concrete cleaner or a variety of other chemicals (page 78). For protection against staining, seal masonry surfaces with clear sealant (pages 54 to 55).

Isolated cracks occur on many concrete building projects. Fill small cracks with concrete caulk or crack-filler (page 44), and patch large cracks with vinyl-reinforced patching material (pages 45 to 47).

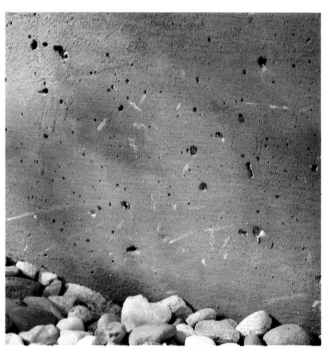

Popouts can be caused by freezing moisture or stress, but very often they occur because the concrete surface was improperly floated or cured, causing the aggregate near the surface of the concrete to loosen. A few scattered popouts do not require attention, but if they are very large or widespread, you can repair them as you would repair holes (pages 46 to 47).

Spalling is surface deterioration of concrete. Spalling is caused by overfloating, which draws too much water to the surface, causing it to weaken and peel off over time. When spalling occurs, it is usually widespread, and the structure may need resurfacing.

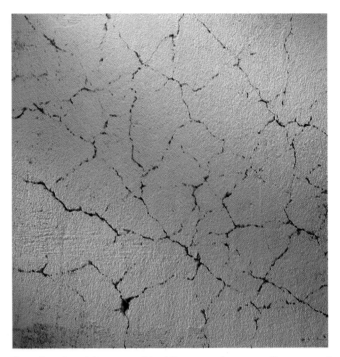

Crazing is widespread hairline cracks, usually caused by overfloating. Clean and seal the surface to help prevent further crazing. For a long-term solution, resurface (pages 48 to 49).

Filling Cracks

The materials and methods you will use for repairing cracks in concrete depend on the location and size of the crack. For small cracks (less than ¼" wide), you can use gray-tinted concrete caulk for a quick fix. For more permanent solutions, use pourable crack filler or fortified patching cements (page 41). The patching cements are polymer compounds that significantly increase the bonding properties of cement, and also allow some flexibility. For larger cracks on flat surfaces, use fortified sand-mix concrete, and for cracks on vertical surfaces, use hydraulic or quick-setting cement. Thorough preparation of the cracked surface is essential for creating a good bonding surface.

Everything You Need:
Tools: wire brush, drill with wire wheel attachment, cold chisel, hand maul, paint brush, trowel.
Materials: vinyl-reinforced patching compound, concrete caulk, sand-mix concrete.

Use concrete repair caulk for quick-fix repairs to minor cracks. Although convenient, repair caulk should be viewed only as a short-term solution to improve appearance and help prevent further damage from water penetration.

Tips for Preparing Cracked Concrete for Repair

Clean loose material from the crack using a wire brush, or a portable drill with a wire wheel attachment. Loose material or debris left in the crack will result in a poor bond and an ineffective repair.

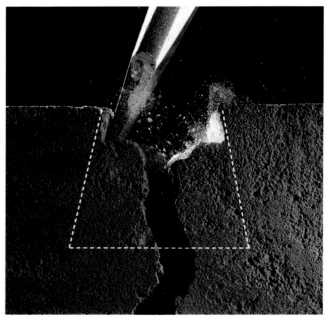

Chisel out the crack to create a backward-angled cut (wider at the base than at the surface), using a cold chisel and hammer. The angled cutout shape prevents the repair material from pushing out of the crack.

How to Repair Small Cracks

1 Prepare the crack for the repair (see previous page), then apply a thin layer of bonding adhesive to the entire repair area, using a paint brush. The bonding adhesive helps keep the repair material from loosening or popping out of the crack.

2 Mix vinyl-reinforced patching compound, and trowel it into the crack. "Feather" the repair with a trowel, so it is even with the surrounding surface.

Variations for Repairing Large Cracks

Sand

Shown cutaway

Horizontal surfaces: Prepare the crack (previous page), then pour sand into the crack to within ½" of the surface. Prepare sand-mix concrete, adding a concrete fortifier, then trowel the mixture into the crack. Feather until even with the surface, using a trowel.

Vertical surfaces: Prepare the crack (previous page). Mix vinyl-reinforced concrete or hydraulic cement, then trowel a ¼" to ½"-thick layer into the crack until the crack is slightly overfilled, and let it dry. Feather even with surface. If the crack is deep (over ½" thick), trowel in consecutive layers, ¼" to ½" thick. Pack in the concrete, let it dry, then pack in more.

Use hydraulic cement or quick-setting cement for repairing holes and chip-outs in vertical surfaces. Because they set up in just a few minutes, these products can be shaped to fill in holes without the need for forms. If the structure is exposed constantly to moisture, use hydraulic cement.

Patching Holes

Large and small holes are treated differently when repairing concrete. The best product for filling in smaller holes (less than ½" deep) is vinyl-reinforced concrete patcher. Because reinforced repair products should be applied only in layers that are ½" thick or less, use sand-mix concrete with an acrylic or latex fortifier for holes more than ½" deep. Sand mix can be applied in layers up to 2" thick.

Patches in concrete will be more effective if you create clean, backward-angled cuts (page 44) around the damaged area, so the repair will bond. For extensive cutting of concrete, use power tools with masonry blades.

> **Everything You Need:**
>
> Tools: trowels, drill with masonry-grinding disc, circular saw with masonry-cutting blade, cold chisel, hand maul, paint brush, screed board, wood float.
>
> Materials: gloves, hydraulic cement, concrete bonding adhesive, vinyl-reinforced patching compound, sand-mix, concrete fortifier.

Tips for Preparing Holes for Repair

For small holes: Cut out around the damaged area with a masonry-grinding disc mounted on a portable drill (or use a hammer and cold chisel). The cuts should bevel about 15° away from the center of the damaged area. Chisel out any loose concrete within the repair area. Always wear gloves and eye protection.

For large holes: Mark straight cutting lines around the damaged area, then cut with a circular saw equipped with a masonry-cutting blade. Set the foot of the saw so the cut bevels away from the damage at a 15° angle. Chisel out any remaining concrete within the repair area. TIP: Set the foot of the saw on a thin board to protect it from the concrete.

How to Repair Small Holes

1 Prepare the damaged area (previous page), then apply a thin layer of bonding adhesive to help create a sturdy bond with the patch.

2 Fill the damaged area with vinyl-reinforced patching compound, applied in layers no thicker than ¼ to ½". Add layers of patching mixture until the hole is filled just above surface level, waiting about 30 minutes between coats. Feather out the surface and let the repair cure.

How to Repair Large Holes

1 Prepare the damaged area (previous page). Mix sand-mix concrete with concrete acrylic fortifier, and fill the damaged area slightly above the surrounding surface.

2 Smooth out and feather the repair with a wood float until the repair is level with the surrounding surface. Re-create any surface finish, like brooming (page 22), used on the original surface.

Resurfacing Concrete

Concrete that has surface damage but is still structurally sound can be preserved by resurfacing—applying a thin layer of new concrete over the old surface. If the old surface has deep cracks or extensive damage, resurfacing will only solve the problem temporarily. A bonding agent helps the new surface adhere to the old. Because new concrete will bond to the old surface better if it is packed down, use a dry, stiff concrete mixture that can be compacted with a shovel.

New surface

Old surface

Shown cutaway

Resurface concrete that has extensive surface damage, like spalling or popouts. Because the new surface is so thin (1" to 2"), use sand-mix concrete. If you are having ready-mix concrete delivered by a concrete contractor, make sure they do not use aggregate larger than ½" in the mixture.

How to Resurface Concrete

1 Clean the surface thoroughly. If the surface is flaking or spalled, scrape it with a spade to dislodge as much loose concrete as you can, then sweep the surface clean.

2 Dig a 6"-wide trench around the surface on all sides to create room for 2 × 4 forms.

3 Stake 2 × 4 forms flush against the sides of the concrete slabs, 1" to 2" above the surface (make sure height is even). Drive stakes every 3 ft., and at every joint in forms. Mark control joint locations onto the outside of the forms, directly above existing control joints. Coat the inside edges of the forms with vegetable oil.

4 Apply a thin layer of bonding adhesive over the entire surface. Follow the directions on the bonding adhesive product carefully. Instructions for similar products may differ slightly.

5 Mix concrete (page 10), using sand-mix concrete. Make the mixture slightly stiffer (drier) than normal concrete (page 8). Spread the concrete, then press down on the concrete with a shovel or 2 × 4 to pack the mixture into the forms. Smooth the surface with a screed board.

6 Float the concrete with a wood float, then tool with an edger (page 21). Recreate any surface treatment, like brooming (page 22), used on the original surface. Cut control joints in the original locations (page 21). Let the surface cure for one week, covered with plastic.

Repairing Steps

Steps require more maintenance and repair than other concrete structures around the house because heavy use makes them more susceptible to damage. Horizontal surfaces on steps can be treated using the same products and techniques used on other masonry surfaces (pages 44 to 47). For vertical surfaces, use quick-setting cement, and shape it to fit.

Everything You Need:

Tools: trowel, wire brush, paint brush, circular saw with masonry-cutting blade, chisel, wood float, edger.

Materials: gloves, bonding adhesive, vinyl-reinforced patching compound, quick-setting cement.

Wear and tear on the surfaces of steps, like the deep popout being repaired above, can be fixed successfully to renew your steps. If you have extensive damage, you may need to replace the steps (pages 30 to 35).

How to Replace a Step Corner

1 Retrieve the broken corner, then clean it and the mating surface using a wire brush. Apply bonding adhesive to both surfaces. If you do not have the broken piece, you can rebuild the corner with quick-setting cement (see next page).

2 Spread a heavy layer of fortified patching cement on the surfaces to be joined, then press the broken piece into position. Lean a heavy brick or block against the repair until the patching compound sets (about 30 minutes). Protect the repair from traffic for at least one week.

How to Patch Step Treads

1 Make a cut in the stair tread just outside the damaged area, using a circular saw with a masonry-cutting blade. Make the cut so it angles toward the back of the step (page 44). Make a similar cut on the riser below the damaged area, then chisel out the area in between the two cuts.

2 Cut a form board the same height as the step riser. Press it against the riser of the damaged step, and brace it in position with heavy blocks. Make sure the top of the form is flush with the top of the step tread.

3 Apply bonding adhesive to the repair area, then press a stiff mixture of quick-setting cement into the damaged area with a trowel.

4 Smooth off the concrete with a wood float, and let it set for a few minutes. Round over the front edge of the nose with an edger. Use a trowel to slice off the sides of the patch, so it is flush with the side of the steps. Wait at least overnight before allowing traffic on the step.

Reset loose masonry anchors by removing the anchors, filling the old holes with anchoring cement (anchoring cement expands as it dries, creating a tighter repair), then pressing the anchors into the fresh cement. Make sure the anchors are not disturbed while the cement sets up (usually about 1 hour).

Miscellaneous Concrete Repairs

There are plenty of concrete problems you may encounter around your house that are not specifically addressed in many repair manuals. These miscellaneous repairs include such tasks as resetting posts and post anchors, patching contoured objects that have been damaged, and repairing masonry veneer around the foundation of your house. You can adapt basic concrete-repair techniques to make just about any type of concrete repair.

Everything You Need:

Tools: putty knife, trowel, hand maul, chisel, wire brush, aviator snips, drill, whisk broom.

Materials: gloves, anchoring cement, quick-setting cement, emery paper, wire lath, concrete acrylic fortifier, sand-mix.

How to Repair Shaped Concrete

1 Scrape all loose material and debris from the damaged area, then wipe down with water. Mix and trowel quick-setting cement into the area. Work quickly—you only have a few minutes before the concrete sets up

2 Use the trowel or putty knives to mold the concrete to follow the form of the object being repaired. Smooth the concrete as soon as it sets up. Buff with emery paper to smooth out any ridges after the repair dries.

How to Repair Masonry Veneer

1 Chip off the crumbled, loose, or deteriorated veneer from the wall, using a cold chisel and hammer. Chisel away damaged veneer until you have only good, solid surface remaining. Use care to avoid damaging the wall behind the veneer. Clean the repair area with a wire brush.

2 Clean up any metal lath in the repair area if it is in good condition. If not, cut it out with aviator snips. Add new lath where needed, using masonry anchors to hold it to the wall.

3 Mix fortified sand-mix concrete (or specialty concrete blends for wall repair), and trowel it over the lath until it is even with the surrounding surfaces.

4 Recreate the surface texture to match the surrounding area. For our project, we used a stiff-bristled brush to stipple the surface. OPTION: To blend in the repair, add pigment to the sand mixture or paint the repair area after it dries (page 41).

Sealing & Maintaining Concrete

Protect concrete that is exposed to heavy traffic or constant moisture by sealing it with a clear concrete sealer. In addition to sealer, there are other special-purpose products designed for concrete surfaces. Specially formulated concrete paints, for example, help keep minerals in the concrete from leeching through paint and hardening into a white, dusty film (called efflorescence).

Regular cleaning is an important element of concrete maintenance to prevent deterioration from oils and deicing salts. Use concrete cleaner products for scheduled cleanings, and special solutions (page 78) for specific types of stains.

Everything You Need:

Tools: paint brush, paint roller and tray, dust brush and pan, caulk gun, paint pad.

Materials: masonry paint, paint thinner, repair caulk, sealer, concrete recoating product.

Use waterproof concrete paint to paint concrete surfaces. Concrete paint is formulated to resist chalking and efflorescence. It is sold in several stock colors, or you can have custom colors mixed from a tint base.

Tips for Cleaning & Maintaining Concrete

Clean oil stains by dampening sawdust with paint thinner, then applying the sawdust over the stain. The paint thinner will break apart the stain, allowing the oil to be absorbed by the sawdust. Wipe up with a broom when finished, and reapply as necessary.

Fill control joints in sidewalks, driveways and other concrete surfaces with concrete repair caulk. The caulk fills the joint, preventing water from accumulating and causing damage to the concrete.

Exposed-aggregate sealer is specially formulated to keep aggregate from loosening. It should be applied about 3 weeks after the concrete surface is poured. To apply, wash the surface thoroughly and allow it to dry. Pour some sealer into a roller tray. Make a puddle of sealer in the corner and spread it out evenly with a paint roller and extension pole.

Clear concrete sealer helps create a water-resistant seal on the surface. The more popular concrete sealing products today are acrylic based and do not attract dirt. Some types of sealer, like the product shown (right), als help the concrete cure evenly.

Masonry recoating products are applied like paint, but they look like fresh concrete when they dry. They are used frequently to improve the appearance of walls, although they generally have little value as waterproofing agents.

Brick and block are easy to work with if you have the right tools and use good techniques. For small jobs, cutting can be done with a mason's chisel and hammer (above). For larger cutting projects, use a circular saw with a masonry-cutting blade to score the bricks or blocks (page 58), or have the masonry units cut to size at a brick yard. TIP: To avoid cracking bricks when cutting, set them on a bed of sand.

Brick & Block Basics

Before starting a brick and block project, familiarize yourself with the handling skills for these materials, shown on the next few pages.

Cutting brick or block is a basic skill you will need to learn before beginning any brick or block building project. Make practice cuts on a few samples to determine how the materials respond to different cutting techniques. Bricks and blocks vary in density and the type of materials used to make them, which greatly affects how they respond to cutting. Testing the water absorption rate (next page) is a good way to evaluate the density of the masonry unit.

In addition to cutting, practice your brick and block stacking techniques (next page) to get a feel for working with the type of masonry unit you will be using. Be sure to buy extra brick and block for every project so you can practice cutting and stacking.

Use bricks tongs to carry several bricks at one time, saving time and preventing damage to bricks. Tongs are sold at brick yards and building centers.

Tips for Working with Brick

Make practice runs on a 2 × 4 to help you perfect your mortar-throwing (pages 60 to 61) and bricklaying techniques. You can clean and reuse the bricks to make many practice runs if you find it helpful, but do not reuse the bricks in your actual project—old mortar can impede bonding.

Test the water absorption rate of bricks to determine density. Squeeze out 20 drops of water in the same spot on the surface of the brick. If the surface is completely dry after 60 seconds, predampen the bricks with water before you lay them to prevent the dry brick from leeching the moisture out of the mortar before it has a chance to set properly.

Tips for Marking Bricks & Blocks

Use a T-square and pencil to mark several bricks for cutting. Make sure the ends of the bricks are all aligned.

Mark angled cuts by dry-laying the project (as shown with concrete pavers above) and setting the brick or block in position, allowing for ⅜" mortar joints when necessary. Mark cutting lines with a pencil, using a straightedge where practical to ensure that cutting lines are straight.

How to Score & Cut Brick

Use a mason's chisel and hammer to score all four sides of the brick when cuts fall over the web area, and not over the core (as shown on page 56, top). Tap on the mason's chisel to leave scored cutting marks about ⅛" to ¼" deep.

Use a circular saw with a masonry-cutting blade to gang-cut bricks or blocks along cutting lines, ensuring uniformity and speeding up the process. Clamp the bricks securely at each end with a pipe clamp or bar clamp, making sure the ends are aligned. Split the bricks, using a mason's chisel and a hammer. NOTE: Wear eye protection when cutting masonry units.

How to Angle-cut Brick

Pivot point

Cutting marks

1 Mark a cutting line on the brick, then score a straight line in the waste area of the brick about ⅛" away from the starting point of the cutting line, perpendicular to the side of the brick.

2 To avoid ruining the brick, you will need to make gradual cuts. Keep the chisel stationary at the point of the first cut, pivot it slightly, then score and cut again. It is important to keep the pivot point of the chisel at the edge of the brick. Repeat until all of the waste area is removed.

How to Cut Brick with a Brick Splitter

1 The brick splitter is a tool that makes accurate, consistent cuts in brick and pavers. It is a good idea to rent one if your project requires many cuts. To use the brick splitter, first mark a cutting line on the brick, then set the brick on the table of the splitter, aligning the cutting line with the cutting blade on the tool.

2 Once the brick is in position on the splitter table, pull down sharply on the handle. The cutting blade on the splitter will cleave the brick along the cutting line. TIP: For efficiency, mark cutting lines on several bricks at the same time (see page 57).

How to Cut Concrete Block

1 Mark cutting lines on both faces of the block, then score ⅛" to ¼"-deep cuts along the lines with a circular saw equipped with a masonry blade.

2 Use a mason's chisel and hammer to split one face of the block along the cutting line. Turn the block over and split the other face.

OPTION: Cut half blocks from combination corner blocks. Corner blocks have preformed cores in the center of the web. Score lightly above the core, then rap with a mason's chisel to break off half blocks.

Mixing & Throwing Mortar

Watching a professional brick-layer at work is an impressive sight, even for do-it-yourselfers who have accomplished numerous masonry projects successfully. The mortar practically flies off the trowel and always seems to end up in perfect position to accept the next brick or block.

Although "throwing mortar" is an acquired skill that takes years of practice to perfect, a beginning bricklayer can use the basic techniques successfully with just a little practice.

The first critical element to handling mortar effectively is the mixture. If the mortar is too thick, it will fall off the trowel in a heap, not in the smooth line that is the goal of throwing mortar. If it is too watery, the mortar is impossible to control and will simply make a mess. Experiment with different water ratios until you find the perfect mixture that will cling to the trowel just long enough for you to deliver it in a controlled, even line that holds its shape after settling. Take careful notes on how much water you add to each batch, then write down the best mixture for your records.

Do not mix more mortar than you can use in 30 minutes. Once mortar begins to set up, it is difficult to work with and yields poor results.

Throwing mortar is a quick, smooth technique that requires practice. Load the trowel with mortar (steps 2 and 3, next page), then position the trowel a few inches above the starting point. In one motion, begin turning your wrist over and quickly move the trowel across the surface to spread mortar consistently. Proper mortar-throwing results in a rounded line about 2½" wide and about 2 ft. long.

Everything You Need:

Tools: trowel, hoe, shovel.

Materials: mortar mix, mortar box, plywood.

How to Mix & Throw Mortar

1 Empty mortar mix into a mortar box and form a depression in the center. Add about three-fourths of the recommended amount of water into the depression, then mix it in with a masonry hoe. Do not overwork the mortar. Continue adding small amounts of water and mixing until the mortar reaches the proper consistency. Do not mix too much mortar at one time—mortar is much easier to work with when it is fresh.

2 Set a piece of plywood on blocks at a convenient height, and place a shovelful of mortar onto the surface. Slice off a strip of mortar from the pile, using the edge of your mason's trowel. Slip the trowel point-first under the section of mortar and lift up.

3 Snap the trowel gently downward to dislodge excess mortar clinging to the edges. Position the trowel at the starting point, and "throw" a line of mortar onto the building surface (see technique photos, previous page). A good amount is enough to set three bricks. Do not get ahead of yourself. If you throw too much mortar, it will set before you are ready.

4 "Furrow" the mortar line by dragging the point of the trowel through the center of the mortar line in a slight back-and-forth motion. Furrowing helps distribute the mortar evenly.

Laying Brick & Block

Patience, care, and good brick-laying techniques are the key elements to building brick and block structures with a professional appearance.

This section features two demonstration projects, a concrete block wall and a brick wall, that show the two basic methods you can follow when building with brick and block. In the block project, the courses are built one at a time; in the brick project, the ends are constructed, then the interior bricks are filled in.

Make sure to have a sturdy, level building surface before you start.

Everything You Need:

Tools: gloves, trowel, chalk-line, level, mason's string.

Materials: mortar mix, 6 × 6" concrete block.

"Buttering" is a term used to describe the process of applying mortar to a brick or block before adding it to the structure being built. For bricks, apply a heavy layer of mortar to one end, then cut off the excess with a trowel. For concrete blocks (inset), apply a mortar line on each of the flanges at one end.

How to Lay Concrete Block

1 Dry-lay the first course, leaving a ⅜" gap between blocks (page 66). Draw reference lines on the concrete base to mark the ends of the row, extending the lines well past the edges of the block. Use a chalkline to snap reference lines on each side of the base, 3" from the blocks. These reference lines will serve as a guide when setting the blocks into mortar.

2 Dampen the base slightly, then mix mortar and throw and furrow two mortar lines (page 61) at one end to create a mortar bed for the combination corner block. Dampen porous blocks (page 57) before setting them into the mortar beds.

3 Set a combination corner block (which has one smooth end) into the mortar bed. Press it into the mortar to create a ⅜"-thick bed joint. Hold the block in place and cut away the excess mortar (save excess mortar for the next section of the mortar bed). Check the block with a level to make sure it is level and plumb. Make any necessary adjustments by rapping on the high side with the handle of a trowel. Be careful not to displace too much mortar.

4 Drive a stake at each end of the project and attach one end of a mason's string to each stake. Thread a line level onto the string and adjust the string until it is level and flush with the top of the corner block. Throw a mortar bed and set a corner block at the other end. Adjust the block so it is plumb and level, making sure it is aligned with the mason's string.

5 Throw a mortar bed for the second block at one end of the project: butter one end of a standard block (page 62) and set it next to the corner block, pressing the two blocks together so the joint between them is ⅜" thick. Tap the block with the handle of a trowel to set it, and adjust the block until it is even with the mason's string. Be careful to maintain the ⅜" joint.

6 Install all but the last block in the first course, working from the ends toward the middle. Align the blocks with the mason's string. Clean excess mortar from the base before it hardens.

(continued next page)

7 Butter the flanges on both ends of a standard block for use as the "closure block" in the course. Slide the closure block into the gap between blocks, keeping the mortar joints an even thickness on each side. Align the block with the mason's string.

8 Apply a 1"-thick mortar bed for the half block at one end of the wall, then begin the second course with a half block.

9 Set the half block into the mortar bed with the smooth surfaces facing out. Use the level to make sure the half block is plumb with the first corner block, then check to make sure it is level. Adjust as needed. Install a half block at the other end.

VARIATION: If your wall has a corner, begin the second course with a full-sized end block that spans the vertical joint formed where the two walls meet. This layout creates and maintains a running bond for the wall.

10 Attach a mason's string for reference, securing it either with line blocks (page 5) or a nail. If you do not have line blocks, insert a nail into the wet mortar at each end of the wall, then wind the mason's string around and up to the top corner of the second course as shown above. Connect both ends and draw the mason's string taut. Throw a mortar bed for the next block, then fill out the second course, using the mason's string as a reference line.

11 Every half-hour, tool the fresh mortar joints with a jointing tool and remove any excess mortar. Tool the horizontal joints first, then the vertical joints. Cut off excess mortar, using a trowel blade. When the mortar has set, but is not too hard, brush any excess mortar from the brick faces. Continue building the wall until it is complete.

OPTION: When building stack bond walls with vertical joints that are in alignment, use wire reinforcing strips in the mortar beds every second or third course (or as required by local codes) to increase the strength of the wall. The wire should be completely embedded in the mortar. Always check with your local building inspector to determine reinforcement requirements, if any.

12 Install a wall cap on top of the wall to cover the empty spaces and create a finished appearance. Set the cap pieces into mortar beds, then butter an end with mortar. Level the cap, then tool to match the joints in the rest of the wall.

Tips for Planning a Brick Wall

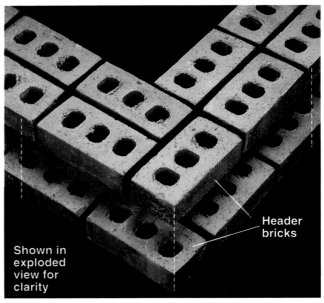

Dry-lay the first course of the wall to test your layout. If you are building a double-wythe wall, the wythes should be ¾" to 1" apart for most walls. Use a chalkline to outline the location of the wall on the slab. Draw pencil lines on the slab to mark the ends of the bricks. Test-fit spacing with a ⅜"-diameter dowel, then mark the location of joint gaps to maintain a reference after the spacers are removed.

To build corners for a double-wythe wall, lay a header brick at the end of two parallel wythes, then reverse the position of the header brick on the next course so it is perpendicular to the first header brick. Continue alternating the pattern all the way to the top of the wall.

How to Build a Double-wythe Brick Wall

1 Dampen the concrete slab or footing with water, and dampen the bricks or blocks if they are porous (page 57, top). Mix mortar and throw a mortar bed (page 61) for the first two bricks of one of the wythes. Butter the inside end of the first brick, then press the brick into the mortar, creating a ⅜" mortar bed. Cut away excess mortar.

2 Plumb the face of the end brick, using a level. Tap lightly with the handle of the trowel to correct the brick if it is not plumb. Level the brick end to end. Butter the end of a second brick (page 62), then set it into the mortar bed, pushing it toward the first brick to create a joint of ⅜".

3 Butter and place a third brick, using the chalklines as a general reference, then using a level to check for level and plumb. Adjust any bricks that are not aligned by tapping lightly with the trowel handle.

4 Lay the first three bricks for the other wythe, parallel to the first wythe. Use a level to level the wythes, and make sure the end bricks and mortar joints align. Fill the gaps between the wythes at each end with mortar.

5 Cut a half brick (page 58), then throw and furrow a mortar bed (pages 60 to 61) for a half brick on top of the first course. Butter the end of the half brick with mortar, then set the half brick in the mortar bed, creating a ⅜" joint. Cut away excess mortar. Check with a level to make sure bricks are plumb and level.

6 Add more bricks and half bricks to both wythes of the corner until you finish the fourth course. Check the corner frequently with a level to make sure it is level and plumb. Align bricks with the reference lines (page 66).

(continued next page)

7 Check the spacing of the end bricks with a straight-edge. Properly spaced bricks will form a straight line when you place the straightedge over the stepped end bricks. If bricks are not in alignment, do not move those bricks already set. Try to compensate for the problem gradually as you fill in the middle (field) bricks by slightly reducing or increasing the spacing between the joints.

8 Every 30 minutes, stop laying bricks and smooth out all the untooled mortar joints with a jointing tool. Do the horizontal joints first, then the vertical joints. Cut away any excess mortar pressed from the joints, using a trowel. When the mortar has set, but is not too hard, brush any excess mortar from the brick faces.

Line block

9 Build the opposite end of the wall with the same methods as the first, using the chalklines as a reference. Stretch a mason's string between the two ends to establish a flush, level line between ends—use a line block to secure the string (page 5). Tighten the string until it is taut. Begin to fill in the field bricks (the bricks between corners) on the first course, using the mason's string as a guide.

10 Lay remaining bricks in the field course. The last brick, called the closure brick, should be buttered at both ends. Center the closure brick between the two adjoining bricks, then set in place with the trowel handle. Fill in the first three courses of each wythe, moving the mason's string up one course after completing each course.

Metal wall tie

11 In the fourth course, set metal wall ties into the mortar bed of one wythe and on top of the brick adjacent to it. Space the ties 2 ft. apart, every three or four courses. For added strength, set metal rebar into the cavities between the wythes and fill with thin mortar.

12 Fill in the remaining courses. Cut away excess mortar. Check the mason's string frequently for alignment, and use a level to make sure the wall stays plumb and level.

13 Lay a furrowed mortar bed on the top course, and place a wall cap on top of the wall to cover empty spaces and provide a finished appearance. Remove any excess mortar. Make sure the cap blocks are aligned and level. Fill the joints between cap blocks with mortar.

Choose the best materials and techniques for repairing problems with brick and block structures. A simple chip or popout, like the one shown above, can be fixed easily by packing the damaged area with latex-fortified mortar. More extensive problems require more complicated solutions.

Repairing Brick & Block Structures

Brick, block, and mortar are very durable building materials. But when they are combined in a permanent structure, stress and the forces of nature can lead to damage that requires attention. Common examples of brick and block structural problems include walls with failing mortar joints, cracked or crumbling bricks or blocks, and worn or discolored surfaces.

Many common brick and block problems can be corrected with simple repairs. These require just a few basic masonry tools (see opposite page) and a minimal investment of time and money. The completed repair job will result in a dramatic improvement in the appearance and strength of the structure. With regular maintenance and cleaning, the repaired structure will provide many years of productive use.

Brick and block are used frequently in the construction of foundation walls, retaining walls, and other load-bearing structures. Some simple repairs, like filling cracks, can be done with a low level of risk. But always get a professional evaluation from a masonry contractor before you attempt to make any major repairs to structures of this type.

This section shows:
• Identifying Brick & Block Problems
  (pages 72 to 73)
• Repairing Brick & Block Walls
  (pages 74 to 77)
• Cleaning & Painting Brick & Block
  (page 78)

Tools for Repairing Brick & Block Structures

Basic tools for repairing brick and block include: a masonry chisel (A) for cutting new brick or block; a cold chisel (B) for breaking up and repairing masonry structures; a raking tool (C) for cleaning mortar out of joints; a mason's trowel (D) for applying mortar to con-crete block; a pointing trowel (E) for applying mortar to brick or block, and for smoothing out fresh repairs; a bricklayer's hammer (F); a ½"-wide (G) and ⅜"-wide (H) joint filler for packing fresh mortar into joints; and a V-shaped mortar tool (I) for finishing mortar joints.

Tips for Working with Mortar

Add concrete fortifier to mortar for making repairs. Fortifier, usually acrylic or latex based, increases overall strength and bondability of mortar.

Add mortar pigment to plain mortar so repairs blend in better. Compare pigment samples, available from concrete products suppliers, to match mortar colors.

Identifying Brick & Block Problems

Inspect damaged brick and block structures closely before you begin any repair work. Accurately identifying the nature and cause of the damage is an important step before choosing the best solution for the problem.

Look for obvious clues, like overgrown tree roots, or damaged gutters that let water drain onto masonry surfaces. Also check the slope of the adjacent landscape; it may need to be regraded to direct water away from a brick or block wall (see *Landscape Construction & Design,* Black & Decker Home Improvement Library), or consult a landscape architect.

Repairs fail when the original source of the problem is not eliminated prior to making the repair. When a concrete patch separates, for example, it means that the opposing stresses causing the crack are still at work on the structure. Find and correct the cause (often a failing subbase or stress from water or freezing and thawing), then redo the repair.

Deteriorated mortar joints are common problems in brick and block structures—mortar is softer than most bricks or blocks, and is more prone to damage. Deterioration is not always visible, so probe surrounding joints with a screwdriver to see if they are sound. Tuckpoint deteriorated joints (page 75).

Major structural damage, like the damage to this brick porch, usually requires removal of the existing structure, making subbase improvements, and reconstruction of the structure. Projects of this nature should only be attempted by professional masons.

Damage to concrete blocks often results from repeated freezing and thawing of moisture trapped in the wall or in the blocks themselves. Instead of replacing the whole block, repair the damaged concrete block or blocks by chipping out the face of the block and replacing it with a concrete paver with the same dimensions as the face of the block.

Spalling occurs when freezing water or other forces cause enough directional pressure to fracture a brick. The best solution is to replace the entire brick (pages 76 to 77) while eliminating the source of the pressure, if possible. Spalled blocks can be refaced (previous photo). TIP: Chip off a piece of the damaged brick to use as a color reference when looking for a replacement.

Damaged mortar caps on chimneys allow water into the flue area, where it can damage the chimney and even the roof or interior walls. Small-scale damage (top photo) can be patched with fire-rated silicone caulk. If damage is extensive (bottom photo), repair or replace the mortar cap.

Stains and discoloration can be caused by external sources or by minerals leeching to the surface from within the brick or block (called efflorescence). If the stain does not wash away easily with water, use a cleaning solution (page 78).

Before **After**

Make timely repairs to brick and block structures. Tuckpointing deteriorated mortar joints (photos above) is a common repair that, like other types of repair, improves the appearance of the structure or surface and helps prevent further damage.

Repairing Brick & Block Walls

The most common brick and block wall repair is tuckpointing—the process of replacing failed mortar joints with fresh mortar. Tuckpointing is a highly useful repair technique for any home-owner. It can be used to repair walls, chimneys, brick veneer, or any other structure where the bricks or blocks are bonded with mortar.

Minor cosmetic repairs can be attempted on any type of wall, from free-standing garden walls to block foundations. Filling minor cracks with caulk or repair compound, and patching popouts or chips are good examples of minor repairs. Consult a professional before attempting any major repairs, like replacing brick or blocks, or rebuilding a structure—especially if you are dealing with a load-bearing structure.

Basement walls are a frequent trouble area for homeowners. Constant moisture and stress created by ground contact can cause leaks, bowing, and paint failure. Small leaks and

cracks can be patched with hydraulic cement. Masonry-based waterproofing products can be applied to give deteriorated walls a fresh appearance. Persistent moisture problems are most often caused by improper grading of soil around the foundation or a malfunctioning downspout and gutter system.

NOTE: The repairs shown in this section feature brick and block walls. The same techniques may be used for other brick and block structures.

Everything You Need:

Tools: raking tool, mortar hawk, joint filler, jointing tool, mason's trowel, mason's chisel, pointing trowel, drill with masonry disc and bit, stiff-bristled brush.

Materials: mortar, gravel, concrete fortifier, replacement bricks or blocks.

How to Tuckpoint Mortar Joints

1 Clean out loose or deteriorated mortar to a depth of ¼" to ¾". Use a mortar raking tool (top) first, then switch to a masonry chisel and a hammer (bottom) if the mortar is stubborn. Clear away all loose debris, and dampen the surface with water before applying fresh mortar.

2 Mix the mortar, adding concrete fortifier. Also add pigment if old mortar joints have discolored (page 71). Load mortar onto a mortar hawk, then push it into the horizontal joints with a joint filler. Apply mortar in ¼"-thick layers, and let each layer dry for 30 minutes before applying another. Fill the joints until the mortar is flush with the face of the brick or block.

3 Apply the first layer of mortar into the vertical joints by scooping mortar onto the back of a joint filler, and pressing it into the joint. Work from the top downward.

4 After the final layer of mortar is applied, smooth the joints with a jointing tool that matches the profile of the old mortar joints. Tool the horizontal joints first. Let the mortar dry until it is crumbly, then brush off the excess mortar with a stiff-bristled brush.

How to Replace a Damaged Brick

1 Score the damaged brick so it will break apart more easily for removal: use a power drill with a masonry-cutting disc to score lines along the surface of the brick and in the mortar joints surrounding the brick.

2 Use a mason's chisel and hammer to break apart the damaged brick along the scored lines. Rap sharply on the chisel with a hammer, being careful not to damage surrounding bricks. TIP: Save fragments to use as a color reference when you shop for replacement bricks.

3 Chisel out any remaining mortar in the cavity, then brush out debris with a stiff-bristled or wire brush to create a clean surface for the new mortar. Rinse the surface of the repair area with water.

4 Mix the mortar for the repair, adding concrete for-tifier to the mixture, and pigment if needed to match old mortar (pages 60 to 61 and 71). Use a pointing trowel to apply a 1"-thick layer of mortar at the bottom and sides of the cavity.

5 Dampen the replacement brick slightly, then apply mortar to the ends and top of the brick. Fit the brick into the cavity and rap it with the handle of the trowel until the face is flush with the surrounding bricks. If needed, press additional mortar into the joints with a pointing trowel.

6 Scrape away excess mortar with a masonry trowel, then smooth the joints with a jointing tool that matches the profile of the surrounding mortar joints. Let the mortar set until crumbly, then brush the joints to remove excess mortar.

For walls with extensive damage, remove bricks from the top down, one row at a time, until the entire damaged area is removed. Replace bricks using the techniques shown above and in the section on building with brick and block (pages 57 to 69). CAUTION: Do not dismantle load-bearing brick structures like foundation walls; consult a professional mason for these repairs.

For walls with internal damaged areas, remove only the damaged section, keeping the upper layers intact if they are in good condition. Do not remove more than four adjacent bricks in one area—if the damaged area is larger, it will require temporary support, which is a job for a professional mason.

Cleaning & Painting Brick & Block

Use a pressure washer to clean large brick and block structures. Pressure washers can be rented from most rental centers. Be sure to obtain detailed operating and safety instructions from the rental agent.

Solvent Solutions for Common Brick & Block Stains

• **Egg splatter:** dissolve oxalic acid crystals in water, following manufacturer's instructions, in a nonmetallic container. Brush onto the surface.

• **Efflorescence:** scrub surface with a stiff-bristled brush. Use a household cleaning solution for surfaces with heavy accumulation.

• **Iron stains:** spray or brush a solution of oxalic acid crystals dissolved in water, following manufacturer's instructions. Apply directly to the stain.

• **Ivy:** cut vines away from the surface (do not pull them off). Let remaining stems dry up, then scrub them off with a stiff-bristled brush and household cleaning solution.

• **Oil:** apply a paste made of mineral spirits and an inert material like sawdust (see page 54).

• **Paint stains:** remove new paint with a solution of trisodium phosphate (TSP) and water, following manufacturer's mixing instructions. Old paint can usually be removed with heavy scrubbing or sandblasting.

• **Plant growth:** use weed killer according to manufacturer's directions.

• **Smoke stains:** scrub surface with household cleanser containing bleach, or use a mixture of ammonia and water.

Check brick and block surfaces annually for stains or discoloration. Most problems are easy to correct if they are treated in a timely fashion. Refer to the information below for cleaning tips that address specific staining problems.

Painted brick and block structures can be spruced up by applying a fresh coat of paint. As with any other painting job, thorough surface preparation and the use of a quality primer are critical to a successful outcome.

Regular maintenance will keep brick and block structures around your house looking their best, helping them last as long as possible.

Tips for Cleaning Masonry

• Always test cleaning solutions on a small area of the surface to evaluate the results.

• Some chemicals and their fumes may be harmful. Be sure to follow manufacturer's safety and use recommendations. Wear protective clothing.

• Soak the surface to be cleaned with water before you apply any solutions. This keeps solutions from soaking in too quickly. Rinse the surface thoroughly after cleaning to wash off any remaining cleaning solution.

Index

Cowles Creative Publishing, Inc.
offers a variety of how-to books.
For information write:
    Cowles Creative Publishing
    Subscriber Books
    5900 Green Oak Drive
    Minnetonka, MN 55343